Sunny Days
Flower Bucket Hat

by

Janis Frank

Table of Contents

I decided to make a new style of bucket hat when I became enamoured with the many granny square hats I was seeing online. While I appreciate the basic granny square, I felt I needed to jazz up the square a bit. I found a very basic flat flower, which I liked, but I knew I could make it a bit nicer with a textured flower and more leaves.

While I wouldn't say that this is a beginner pattern, I've supplied numerous photos to show you how to make all of the more complicated parts. As long as you have the crochet basics down, this pattern should be easy.

The hat itself is made to fit adults and is a one size fits most. It's not too small to fit a larger head (that would be someone like me) but tight enough to be a roomy, easy fit for those with an average size head. I made all of the hats in the photos out of 100% cotton yarn for comfort, but you can use whatever you prefer, or have on hand.

Things You Need

4 colours of worsted weight yarn (center, flower, leaves and hat body and brim). I used 100% cotton yarn for breathability in hot temperatures but you can use anything. You will need at least 2 of the smaller balls of cotton yarn for the main colour. I used the yarn that comes in the large balls of cotton yarn for my main colour.

3.5 mm (size E or 4) crochet hook

Stitch markers – spare pieces of yarn will work.

Tapestry needle to sew seams and work in ends

Gauge

In DC - double crochet

10 sts = 2 inches (5 cm)

5 rows = 2 inches (5 cm)

Each square measures approximately 12 cm (4.75 inches) wide.

This is a fairly densely packed square with more sts per inch. It's not very "floppy" and is more stiff. If you are wanting more flexibility in your final project, like a blanket, use a larger hook, like a 5 mm (Size H or 6) or so.

The Granny Square *(make 5)*

With your choice of center colour,

Ch 2 making first chain large enough to fit the next 8 sts.

Round 1: 8 HDC. Join with sl st at the top of the first ch. Break yarn.

With your choice of flower petal colour,

Round 2: In any HDC, join with sl st. Ch 1 and make it into a large loop. Pull up a large loop. YO. Pull up a loop. YO. Pull up a loop. YO draw through all the loops ion your hook. Ch 2. ♠ In the next HDC, *Pull up a loop. YO* Repeat from * to * 3 times more (total of 4 large loops). Draw through all loops on your hook. Ch 2 ♠ Repeat form ♠ to ♠ around for a total of 8 petals. Join with sl st to the first ch 1 of the first petal. Break yarn. Tie off.

Pull up large loop

Pull up a large loop

YO and pull up a large loop

YO and pull up another loop

YO

Draw through all loops on hook. Ch 2

In next HDC, pull up a loop

YO and pull up loops like you did before

YO and draw through all loops. Ch 2

With your choice of leaf colour,

Round 3: Join with sl st in any Ch 2 space. Ch 1 ♣ YO. Draw up a loop as if to make a DC. YO and draw through the first 2 loops on your hook. Leave the remaining loops on your hook unworked.♣ Repeat from ♣ to ♣ one more time. YO and draw through the all loops on your hook. (Small middle leaf complete). ▲ Ch 4.. In the next Ch 2 space, ♥ ◘ YO 3 times. Draw up a loop as before. YO and draw through the first 2 loops on your hook. YO. Draw through the next 2 loops on your hook. YO Draw through the next 2 loops on your hook. Leave the remaining loops on the hook unworked.◘ Repeat from ◘ to ◘ 2 more times. YO and draw through all 4 loops on your hook. ♥ (1st corner leaf made). Ch 5. Repeat from ♥ to ♥ 1 time staying in the same Ch 5 space of the leaf just made. (2nd corner leaf made). Ch 4. In the next Ch 2 space, Repeat from ♣ to ♣ but repeat *3 times total*. (Small middle leaf made).▲ Repeat from ▲ to ▲ ending with last 2 corner leaves. Ch 4. Join with sl st to the top of 1st small middle leaf. Break yarn. Tie off.

YO and draw through first 2 loops as if
you were going to make a DC.
Leave the 2 loops unworked.

YO

Pull up a loop

YO and draw through the 2 loops. Leave remaining loops unworked.

YO and draw through all loops on hook.

Smaller middle leaf made. Ch 4

YO 3 times

In next ch 2 space, draw up a loop

YO and draw through 1st 2 loops

YO and draw through next 2 loops

YO and draw through next 2 loops. Leave the remaining loops unworked.

In same ch 2 space, YO 3 times to make next "arm" of leaf

YO and draw up a loop. Repeat the leaf "arm" same as last time.

Leave the remaining loops unworked.

Make the 3rd "arm"

YO and draw through the 4 loops on your hook.

Ch 5 and make another leaf in this ch 2 space.

Ch 4. YO and draw up loop in next ch 2 space.

Draw up a loop

YO and draw through 2 loops.

Leave remaining loops unworked

YO and draw up a loop in same ch 2 space

YO and draw through the 2 loops on hook.

Leave remaining st unworked.

YO and draw through all loops on your hook. Ch 4

With your choice of edging colour,

Round 4: Join with sl st in the DC of any small middle leaf, Ch 2. ♫ In the next Ch 4 space, (DC, HDC, SC). SC in each of the next 2 sts. In the Ch 5 corner space, 5 SC, SC in each of the next 2 sts. In the Ch 4 space (SC, HDC, DC) DC in the next 2 sts. ♫ Repeat from ♫ to ♫ ending with 1 DC in the next st. Join with sl st in the top of the starting Ch 2.

Join in this st on ANY small middle leaf

DC, HDC, SC in ch 4 space

SC in next 2 sts

5 SC in ch 5 space between corner leaves

SC next 2 sts

SC, HDC, DC in ch 4 space

DC in next 2 sts of small middle leaf

Round 5: Working evenly over the sts unless otherwise stated, 6 SC, 3 SC in the corner st, ☼ 16 SC, 3 SC in the corner st. ☼ Repeat from ☼ to ☼ 2 more times. 8 SC. Join with sl st in starting SC. Break yarn. Tie off.

Make 4 more granny squares. Join squares together to make a circle. You can sew them together or use a sl st along the edges. Make the seam from middle corner SC to the middle corner SC.

Take a photo of this square for
FREE patterns on my website!

Hat Top

Round 1: With the RIGHT side of the circle facing you, and on either edge, count back 4 sts from any joining seam. Join yarn with a sl st, SC, HDC, DC. Place a st marker at the seam. 18 DC *2DCtog twice. 16 DC. Place st marker on the seam* Repeat from * to * around to the 2 sts before the st marker. Do NOT join! You will now work continuously around the top of the hat.

Count back 4 sts

Join with Sl St, SC, HDC, DC.

Place marker

18 DC

2DCtog in these 2 stitches (decrease)

2DCtog made

2DCtog on other side of the seam

2DCtog at end of round.

Round 2 and beyond: ☺ 2DCtog on each side of the st marker. DC to the 2 sts before the st marker. ☺. Repeat around from ☺ to ☺ until there are no sts between the 2DCtog. Make 2DCtog until there are 6 sts left. HDC over 2 sts. (Pull up loop in next 2 sts. YO and draw through all 3 loops on your hook). Join with a sl st in the next st. Break yarn. Tie off. Work in end.

Hat Brim

Round 1: With the RIGHT side of the hat facing you, count back 4 sts from any joining seam. SC, HDC, DC. Place a st marker at the seam. DC around to st marker. Do NOT join but work in continuous rounds.

Round 2: ◊ 4 DC 2DC in next st. ◊ Repeat around from ◊ to ◊ to the st marker.

Round 3: 8 DC, 2 DC in next st. ♪ 5 DC 2DC in next st. ♪ Repeat around from ♪ to ♪ to the st marker. 2 DC in last st. (don't worry if your off by a few sts).

Round 4: DC around to the st marker. HDC, SC, sl st in the next st to join. Ch 1. Turn.

Round 5: With the WRONG side facing you, SC around to st marker. Join with sl st in Ch 1. Break yarn. Tie off. Work in ends.

Abbreviations

SC – single crochet

DC – double crochet

HDC – half double crochet

2DCtog – crochet 2 sts together. Do **NOT** YO. Pull up a loop in the next st as if to make a SC. Pull up a loop in the next st. YO. Draw through 2 loops on your hook. YO. Draw through the 2 loops on your hook. Decrease made. 2 stitches are now crocheted together.

YO – yarn over

sl st – slip stitch

st – stitch

sts - stitches

Hints and Tips

If counts are off for round 5, SC as many sts as you need to get to the middle st of the corner. Make sure the 3 sts in one st are always in the middle st.

There are a lot of ends when you make a multi-coloured granny square. Work the ends in as you crochet. Hold your yarn to the back of your work and catch the end over a few sts while you crochet. There are lots of great videos online that can show how.

If you would like a wider brim on your hat, DC with increases every other row around. End one row of DC without increases and a row of SC.

If the hat is too big or too small, you can always switch up the hook size. Use a smaller hook to make it smaller, and a larger hook for a bigger one. I wouldn't add or take away a square as they are quite large and will make a big difference in the size. A larger size hook will also make the brim less stiff and more floppy.

Please note I can't help you with sizing if you've changed the hook size.
Like all of my patterns you have my permission to sell and/or give away the physical items that you make using this pattern. You are NOT permitted to reprint this pattern in any form unless you have obtained my written permission to do so.

If you have any questions, please feel free to leave a comment or send me your questions at kweenbee_crafts@hotmail.ca.

Help Support My Work!

Follow me on Instagram, Facebook, Pinterest and YouTube. Every follow, subscribe, thumbs up, like, heart and share help increase my popularity on the web and get more viewers to my work. It costs you nothing but helps me sooooo much!

If you would like to help a little more, you can always become a Website Member to download print over 45 patterns. Or you can support me by becoming a Patron on Patreon or you can make a single time donation at Buy Me a Coffee.

You can use any of these QR codes to find out more.

Website Member

Patreon

Buy Me a Coffee

More FREE patterns on my website

I'm always creating new patterns and I post every one of them over on my website. It is an ever growing list so you might want to check out my page at **KweenBee.com** . I design new patterns as I get time. I aim to add a couple new ones each month so the list is always growing!

Crochet Sun Hat and Bucket Hat

Friendshi and Flower Bracelet

Crochet Slippers for shildren and Adults

Of course,, none of the links will not work. To make it even easier, you can take a photo of the QR code below with your phone or tablet. A link will pop up. Tap that link and it will take you right to the webpage to see all of the patterns including those above.

Follow Me on Social Media

Take a photo with your phone or tablet of the QR codes below. A link will appear. Click the link to go straight to my social media page.

Twitter	YouTube	Threads
Facebook	Instagram	Pinterest
Patreon	My Etsy Shop	Buy Me a Coffee

www.ingramcontent.com/pod-product-compliance
Lightning Source LLC
Chambersburg PA
CBHW081014120626
46546CB00010B/3148